Blowing Up Growing Up

To Cori & Cameron

Thankyou with Lots of Love ♡ ♡

John

Copyright © 2024 John Givins
This work is protected by Canadian copyright law. Except as otherwise provided for under Canadian copyright law, no part of this work may be copied, published, distributed, downloaded or otherwise stored in a retrieval system, transmitted or converted, in any form or by any means, electronic or otherwise, without the prior written permission of the publisher.
No part of this work may be used, read, analyzed, simulated or imitated by any electronic means including, but not limited to, any artificial intelligence engine or computer software without the express written permission of the publisher.
No part of this publication was created or enhanced by use of any form of artificial intelligence.

Published 2024
Askance Publishing
ISBN 978-1-778225-06-2

also available as an ePub

Set in Sabon by Askance Publishing

Photographs used by permission
All rights reserved.

Library and Archives Canada Cataloguing in Publication

Title: Blowing up growing up / by John Givins.
Names: Givins, John, author.
Identifiers: Canadiana (print) 20230620922 | Canadiana (ebook) 2023062250X | ISBN 9781778225062 (softcover) | ISBN 9781778225079 (EPUB)
Subjects: LCGFT: Poetry.
Classification: LCC PS8613.I85 B56 2024 | DDC C811/.6—dc23

WITH GRATITUDE
johngivins@telus.net

Blowing Up Growing Up
by
John Givins

To Trish, I took my time to find you, the love of my life, and Adrian my ace supporter.

A poem is an invitation to a voyage. As in life, we travel to see fresh sights.
― *Charles Simic*

Contents

When I Leave Trish – 1

Love
A Kiss – 4 About 10 PM – 5 First Morning Touch – 6
Kissing In The Car – 7 You Cut My Hair – 8
Your Scarf – 9 Another Kiss – 10

Neighbourhood Perspectives
What House? – 12 Acid Jazz – 13 Autumn Leaves – 14
It's Him Again – 15 Winter Show – 16 Jeanne – 17
November Downpour – 18 June 16th 2011 – 19
Losing My Marbles – 20 Paper Towels – 21
Music To Me – 22 Mattress – 23 Stationwagon – 24
New Year's Eve – 25 Oh Deer – 26 Billboard Man – 27
Revellers at Legion 142 – 28 Roving Prowler – 30
Pennsylvania Hotel – 32

In a Nutshell
Urbanity – 34 Fish – 35 Tomato Paste – 36
Lucky – 37 Green Olives – 38 The Commute – 39
Screams – 40 Lobster – 41 Summer Ferry – 42

Travels
Map of India – 44 En España – 45 Koi – 46
RVing – 47 Marrakesh Market – 48 Morocco – 50
Season Opener March 2020 – 53
Paris Brasserie – 54 Tulum – 55 Subway – 56
Sheepish – 57 Reappearance – 58

Family and Friends
Hey Sweetpea – 60 Heather – 61 Birthday Balloons – 62
Lists – 63 August 16th – 64 Buttons – 66 Maria – 67
Christina Lake – 68 Michael Kerry – 70
Nearly Drowned – 72 Mike Frastacki's Solo Road – 73
Murmuring – 74 Unfortunately – 76 Shyness – 77

Teenage Years – 78   Sweet Jesus – 80
What Are The Chances – 82   The Jones – 84   Dad – 86
My Wife's Sisters – 88   South Carolina – 89

Around the House
Our Clothesline – 92   Bowls – 93
Ants – 94   Her Jewellery Organizer – 96
Folding Laundry – 97   Happy Shoes – 98
Patio Chairs – 99   Illustrious Characters – 100

The Road
Tow Truck Drivers – 104   Bus Shelter – 106
Millennial – 107   "F" – 108   Cardboard – 110
Tandem Exuberance – 111   VW Bug – 112
City Buses – 114   Highway Shrine – 116

From the Bedroom
Early Morning – 120   Insomniac – 121   Pillow Talk – 122
Rock Concert – 123   Sleep Thief – 124

It's a Dog's World
Pup Culture – 126   Rover – 128   Morning News – 129
In The Dog House – 130

Whimsy
Cracked – 132   Church Sign – 133
Gaggling Seagulls – 134   Magazine Aisle – 135
Spinal Tattoo – 136   Saturday Night Swing – 138
The Ventriloquist At The Beach – 139
The Juggler At The Beach – 140
The Pantomime At The Beach – 142
The Clairvoyant Not At The Beach – 143   Two Nuns – 144

Acknowledgements – 147

About the Author – 149

Introduction

I started writing poems in the last six years as a creative escape during my wife's marathon trials with colon cancer. These years have been peppered with bad times and I've rarely written about the arduous specifics of her treatments. During this journey, I have been graced to be at her side and never imagined this process would give me such comfort.

I've aimed at depicting scenes, like nut shells filled with condensed milk, of the beauty of life's mosaic, everyday moments that celebrate the ordinary, recounting my pivotal crazy years, honouring friends who have gone before me and recapturing our fortunate travel experiences.

I've dressed my poems in plain visible clothing, drawing the reader into some details I've seen and worn, growing up in Vancouver. Some came easily, others had to be pickled in a glass jar with special poetry vinegar for weeks and weeks. There are long ones that I couldn't cut shorter and short ones I couldn't make longer.

For my friends, this may be the first poetry book that will grace your home since high school. Billy Collins said about poetry "it doesn't need to be beaten with a garden hose to get the meaning out."

My wife Trish, an incredible editor-in-chief, has dissected and augmented the poems using her finest poetry lice comb, clarifying far more than just checking for commas and capitals, with consideration and care for the reader.

Open it anywhere, there are parts of me inserted here. So, welcome reader, I am happy, grateful and looking forward to sharing this time with you. Words are weak to express my gratitude.

When I Leave Trish

Written in the summer of 2018 during Trish's lengthy hospital stay on the palliative ward.

I leave Trish in the hospital alone; after a day of her being poked, prodded and sedated. It's late.

After a goodnight kiss, one, that like her pain killers, will hopefully last all night, I pack up my bag of unease, my heart in my shoes, and under the harsh chrome fluorescents, float away like an unneeded ghost.

Down the polished terrazzo hallways, now vacated of stressed families, past the nurses' station with real living angels pushing twelve-hour shifts, vigilantly dispensing pain placating pills and a thousand expressions of compassion, supported by attentive care aides.

I pass clusters of stainless steel laundry shelves, sterilized equipment carts and rooms replete with an ever-changing tide of the sick, damaged, diseased and dying; attempting at least a restful sleep, caught in an uncertainty of their mortality, hoping that they'll be better tomorrow.

At the now deserted elevator, a blood red arrow marks *down*, descending through ten floors of fragility and precarious frailty. A medical repair shop for all the intricate puzzle pieces of our marvellous body.

Exiting past the imploring hand sanitizers, I discharge myself through the Don't-Take-The-Germs-Home automatic front doors leaving my day's adventure with my love and take a breath of the crisp fresh night.

I wend past the concrete parkade and cross the street, away from the hospital's dark edifice and asthmatic fans. I float into the warm embrace of an enveloping summer night, rubbing shoulders with the living, and find solace from the neighbouring apartment blocks. Those ones with faded Christmas-lit balconies, abundant flowerpots, rusty bar-b-ques, open windows with cat-tattered blinds and the serenading budgie. They lend me comforting sounds of healthy people watching movies peppered with superstars or the rapid-fire-no-good evening news while waiting for the pizza delivery man. Some share a bottle of red and music with friends while playing with their new baby who won't go to sleep. We all have our stories to tell, our lives to lead and fairness seems to be dispensed indiscriminately.

    I return home with the beat of only one heart, to shower off the stale hospital dross, hoping to put my worry to sleep, holding tightly the pain of love and longing, the sting of love in separation, craving the love of union to dream of Trish receiving those words *you can go home now*: where she belongs. Once again to enjoy her laughter and her touch, to have my woman's warmth lying next to me, kiss her always warm moist lips, to wrap our arms around each other and to wake in the relief of our own soft bed listening to the rhythm of her magical breathing and the big, wonderful heart of my bounce-back girl.

Love

A Kiss

A kiss that is soft
warm and moist
juicy sweet and savoury with love.

I kiss your smile
a bonus.
Your lips tell
me how soft
really soft
slow soft
rolling soft.
Top lip
bottom lip
en español
labios rojos
red lips
that I'll never
be tired of kissing.

About 10 PM

I turn down your bed
and open the window above
so the night air will freshen your sleep
and keep away those nightmares.

Awake at sunrise,
all I can see is your tussled red hair
floating on feather pillows
above the blankets.

I have to pull them back
a little
to see
where the best to kiss.

First Morning Touch

In the early morning stillness
of winter's naked darkness,
eyes closed with sleep
stirring from under a Persian carpet of dreams,
craving the first warm touch of reconnection,
a magic spark of electricity.

Not wanting to wake her,
my hands move slowly as an opening flower
floating feather soft
landing like dust
two souls melting together
wrapped in a comforter of love
exploring favourite and new
secrets of tenderness.

Kissing in the Car
(A Mazda Protegé)

Two lovers close
in a darkened car,
touched by the night streetlight.
Kissing.
Kisses full of love,
kisses with kindness,
connecting sparks inside
with only sounds of
their beating hearts
and warm summer rain
drumming on the roof.

You Cut My Hair

I like to call it silver
but it's really white
except for the brown band
above my neck.
It was scraggly
and you'd wanted to trim it for weeks,
so you cut my hair
with so much care
the mod way that makes you happy.

You said,
"Just thinning it on the sides and
the fuzz on your neck."
I wet my hair,
with the vegetable sprayer
and sat in my underwear
in the centre of the kitchen.

I trusted you
with what to do,
while I clipped my nails after brunch
on that January Sunday
and through a grey comfortless sky
the sun slanted thinly in the clippings
across the maple floor.

Your Scarf

I love seeing you wear your scarf,
the new one
with the ruby red blossoms
and orange leaves
that you bought in Portland
in the store you loved
one out of ten thousand items.

It is delicately light
yet cozy
warming and tender like you
and deliciously attractive
wrapped in an embrace
around your soft neck
covering the history of
my thousand kisses.

Another Kiss

Hey Lucky Lips
is there time in our life
for another kiss?
Maybe a little kiss
or a big kiss?

Yes, you don't have to ask.
Ever.

Silly question.
Golden melting kisses
flowing with love
filling my heart
with velvet touches
of your always warm
juicy, ruby lips.

Neighbourhood Perspectives

What House?

Do we have a soul?
Does the home where we were conceived,
learned to walk, talk, read and tie our shoes have a soul?
Today our family home was reduced to rubble.

Who wants a small old house?
How has time changed this address
once full of hopes and dreams?

After Mom and Dad died
it was rented to university students
then sat vacant, lonely
except for the neighbourhood rats
who had to move too
when an insolent ferocious Dinosaurus Rex,
with insatiable steel jaws devoured it in a dusty cloud
collapsing it efficiently
as would an angry brat pulverize a favourite toy.
The once well-framed walls
of family built stories and a sheltering roof
under which we grew and ricocheted
was splintered, crashed, smashed.
Our garden plants, shrubs and trees
added to the ruins, supplying a rubble industry
creating a land fill mountain by the river.

Mom's favourite appliances were
in a firing line of the wrongly convicted,
the former cement foundation
and the stairs and sidewalk
where we ran and laughed
were pulverized, trucked and dumped
expediently, expendably along the river's breakwater
drowning with it the wealth of our lifetime
and the unaccounted for
soul of our family home.

Acid Jazz

From the stoned chapter of my crazy years
stuck in my memory is an orange tab
courtesy of the White Rabbit
that I took with Mike and Danny
tripping down a laneway off Main Street
to an underground jazz club
packed with Saturday night revellers.

Glasses clinked as the musicians played with notes,
like kids making up games in a playground.
Abstract tunes flowing through
a candlelit white cigarette haze of jazz.

Who really understands this stuff anyway?
I just love listening to it, the drummer feeling his cymbals
a heart-beat base, tickling ivories,
the xylophonist definitely on speed and a sexy sax.

I've been told they're talking to each other,
connecting in their own language.
Musicians comprehend it
with their occult circle of fifths
equalling my knowledge of Kyrgyzstan

At our table in the back corner
we laughed at our best stories
and were the last ones left.
They created one more piece, all out of tune
dedicated to our unique sensibility.

In the early morning we blew out
into the deserted psychedelic streets,
as the musicians poured into a taxi
to their blacks-only hotel.

Autumn Leaves

It's fall.
Leaf falling season from the local trees.

They wave on their stems
where they've been glued all summer
and after a brilliant green performance
their yearly display ends in a symphony of colour
the adhesive loosened by crisp blowing winds
whipping them into a riotous whirlwind dance
falling untethered from their parents
fluttering down to earth.

They're landing on water
and falling on land
enveloping the surface
with sheaves of leaves of letters
that tell grand stories of a refreshing spring start
long sunny summer days and now an autumn glory.

A few at first flutter down
gradually increasing
sporadically all day and night
building up to cascading flurries
of thousands upon thousands
tumbling down like snow
falling like confetti
knowingly relinquishing their splendour
disconnecting from their reason to be green
re-forming into a yellow auburn autumn patchwork quilt.

It's stitched together with invisible stitches
stitched with threads of seasons passing
stitching short crisp days to long chilling nights
stitching a comforter for a wedding
of autumn to winter.

It's Him Again

After the peace of the night has passed
Kevin arrives from where he slept
in the forest by the penitentiary,
racing the sunrise.

He has a lot to say,
a seasoned braggart.
In fact, all his family are big talkers
like some people I know.

I can't understand a thing he says
but it sounds very important
perhaps, who he will meet up with today
or what he might eat.

He likes hopping around in our big trees
then flying away, fanning the airwaves
in his finely tailored black feathered suit
to where, I don't know.

Winter Show

Boulevard trees stand strong
sleeping and still
poised faithfully in rows
between sentinel streetlights,
as their dark silhouetted shadows sway
in the winter ocean mist.
While the lonesome foghorn
blows its two-note lament,
they patiently wait
for the next, yet distant season
to bring them back to life.
Tonight, they dream deep
of a coming spring light
when their great arms will again stretch,
waking, laden with fresh green leaves
that will dance and flutter
in the warm breath of summer.

Jeanne

Strolling up Grand Boulevard,
a woman I never had met,
welcomed me to sit and rest a while.

She was born in the same year as
Shirley MacLaine, John Cleese,
and Donald Duck.

I said to her,
I can see you as the apple of your parent's eyes,
growing to be the peach of your husband's love,
raising the kids through all the stages
all the meals, lessons and praise,
up to raising the last glass.
How does a mother say goodbye?

With its gorgeous view of our changing city,
your park bench plaque proclaimed
"IT'S BEEN A HOOT!
See you over the rainbow."
Jeanne Cordocedo 1934 - 2013.

And from the leaves of a shading tree,
music floated in the summer breeze
singing with your laughter
leaving this wish
from your comforting spirit.

November Downpour

It's pissing out there and
I'm not going outside unless I have to,
falling from gruesome, scudding banks of clouds,
that began without an ending
obscuring drenched, reclining mountains
carpeted with giant cedars, firs, hemlocks,
washing their outstretched green furry arms
waving, wildly waltzing,
like soaking bridal trails,
lapping it up, confessing their love
embraced by easterly blows,
wicking away the last vestiges
of summer's warmth.

It's a blustery cats and dogs day,
horizontal rains
draw sinuous dribble lines down the windows,
from the metal roof above
there's a gaggle of stoned drummers
blending into a monotone
with a distant ship's horn.

Chance of precipitation, 100%.
The tide is coming in
even the ducks
have found shelter.

June 16th 2011

Frenzied mobs have vanished
the smoke has cleared
city clean-up crews with heads down,
do overtime street cleaning.

Vancouver needs a morning-after pill
post nasty Stanley Cup riot.

Behind cracked glass windows
rattled coffee shop patrons
reboot their lives.

Justice ensues with unprecedented
social media participation.

Losing My Marbles

Yesterday, while picking up my wife's meds,
I wandered around in what we know
is a lot more than just a drug store.

I steered clear of the shampoos, makeup,
stationary supplies and gift cards.
Bypassing the attractive braggarts in the magazine aisle,
I wandered with curiosity into the toy aisle.

Amongst the Ultra Clean Washable Rainbow Markers,
packs of 40 Disney Stickers and balloon rockets,
were compact boxes of marbles
with a Norman Rockwell style illustration
of a smug young boy squinting for the right trajectory,
while behind him, kneeling by their draw-string sack
his sister in pig tails, hovers for her turn.

Long ago when Mom dropped me at Primary school,
recess was the best part of the day,
always with matches when one big kid,
also the class bully, would clean up.
Those brave enough to continue playing
returned to class dejected, empty pocketed.

These days I don't take many chances
I don't frequent casinos,
and I try to stay off ladders.

After surviving a wild gamble with my first wife
my second is a jackpot.

At recess, I never lost all my marbles,
especially not the beautiful cat's eyes.
No one wants to feel like a looser
in any school of life.

Paper Towels

I think in every public bathroom
I've used and dried my hands in,
coffee shops, restaurants, offices,
they all have signs, handmade or computer printed
clearly stating:

Please don't put paper towels in the toilet.

...... apparently it needs repeating,
in case you didn't read it in the last bathroom
as if you throw them in your toilet at home
anonymous you, behind the locked door.

Rick, my plumber buddy, says it's like canvas in the pipes,
an unappealing, unenviable clean out job,
shitty bread and butter work
not fun, even for $100 an hour cheque or cash.

In my book, it's most deserving
of a beer or two at the end of the day,
after he's washed his hands.

Music To Me

In a home's front window down the street,
framed by plush curtains,
rests a baby grand piano
enshrined in mahogany and ebony gloss
its lid propped open expectantly.

I pass by repeatedly
but have heard it played only once,
tuning my walk into a rhapsody
of beautiful notes uplifting my steps
accompanying a choir of neighbouring song birds.

It stands there silent, lonesome, patient,
waiting like a thoroughbred for a good run
dreaming of creating music reverberating off the walls.

I wish to knock on their door and play a solo,
pull some sheets from the dusty bench
and play them a Bach fugue, Boogie-Woogie
or perhaps some impromptu jazz
but I could never stick to those exercises,
too distracted to focus on a new language
for even a hundred hours
no do-re-mi for me.

Mattress

On a hot afternoon
I saw two guys
weaving along a crowded sidewalk
beneath tall apartment shadows
carrying a large soft mattress
on their heads.
Western style coolies.

It flopped up and down
waving like a compliant rectangular manta ray
the guy in front stabilizing it
with muscular outstretched arms
the guy in back texting friends
about an imminent
housewarming party.

Stationwagon

When Cathy was a kid
she saw a woman drive by in the stationwagon
her dad had sold last month.

Some woman was driving it
full of kids loaded up for a camping trip
on the same day Dad was to leave for a conference.

Years later, she learned he really did like camping
as well as a hankering for philandering.

New Year's Eve

An hour after midnight
the neighbours are fast asleep
in orderly residential rows
full of those valuing sleep.

Save for the shindig house
on the corner
where loud revellers
pour out onto the street
alcohol and pounding music saturated
a gaggle of 20 somethings
swerving and puking
unsure futurists
stabilized by boulevard trees
pissing on the fence
bragging loud stories of omnipotence
and crazy improbable adventures
of lives to be lived
jobs to be explored
marathons to run
waiting for a cab
to an ambiguous new year.

Oh Deer

Once timid, nimble and balletic,
Bambi's aunt 6th removed
lithely chose the neighbour's woodshed
to curl up in the wood chips and die.

A week later
the evening ocean breeze shifted,
revealing a pungent dead deer smell
rancorously blanketing
the neighbour's summer sunset deck.

Jovial guests,
chipped ice cocktails in hand
hastily dispersed.

Billboard Man

High on his perch above the crowded avenues,
comfortable up and down his ladder
hooking it over the top
safety harnessed in
like a high wire circus act
scraping, tearing last month's advert off.

Enormous thick paper leaves flopping down to earth
in torn swaths, leaving behind a layered abstract
on weathered plywood
an urban pop art exhibit.

I've seen them in Madras,
artists like spiders on bamboo scaffoldings
hand painting larger than life archetypes
Bollywood heroines and villains
messaging escape for the masses below.

This burly billboard man
pulled this month's colossal new ad
from his van, in neatly folded multiple tablecloths.

He roped up his long-handled brush
a classic bucket of glue
and from his perilous landing
wildly sloped it on,
athletically squeegeed, neatly matching up corners,
all the while keeping an eye out
on the sidewalk below for an audience
for any admiring women's glances.

Revellers at Legion 142

After a few beers,
on a visit to the men's washroom
I gaze at a print above the urinal
of a de Havilland Mosquito M14
that my dad maintained, and my uncle flew.

These wood framed pathfinders
flew ahead, dropping flares on enemy targets
for the following bomber squadrons.

Came closing time, an incredulous crew
poured out, parading in arms, into the crisp night
under Broadway's starry streetlights.

The veteran barmaids had homes to go to
shooed us rowdies out back to our sleeping wives.
The band had sung our favourites
and packed up long ago.

I parted from my loosely mustered friends
on a cold Remembrance night
with warm laughs and embraces.

Thinking like marching,
weaving across the intersection,
past the clicking rotational billboard
messaging a persuasive glow
onto the cold sidewalk shadows.

Murmuring traffic, a barking dog,
an incoming jetliner, high overhead
whistling down through the octaves
above the city's peaceful sleepiness.

After so many November 11ths,
the devastating toll of loss
the atrocious consequences
World War I and II and too many others
all for our freedom.

So, we raise our glasses in praise, we the living
in this fortunate life we've inherited.

Roving Prowler

Down the block, a friend's teen daughter was in a car
with her new squeeze, necking under
the summer street light shadows of 3 am.

Later, she professed they were just talking.
Regardless, coming up for air
they saw an oily culprit working the street
checking for unlocked cars
like a salad chef searching
for a ripe avocado.

When I lived on the east side,
I emptied my van and never locked it.
It saved on the deductible for smashed windows
and rarely I would notice someone had slept there.

Admittedly sometimes I forget
to lock our car on this west side.
My forgetfulness, a business opportunity
for this itinerant thief,
and he was feeling lucky
searching for coins, or goods for his sustenance.

The teens watched him and called the Fuzz.
but he slipped away like Wily Coyote.

In the morning I found the thief had dropped
an iPod on my passenger seat
loaded with an interesting array of tunes,
some I liked, others not so much.

I left a note in my car window for weeks,
"To whoever rifled through my car,
that was my cat's catnip you pocketed, not pot.
You've decent taste in music
and if my knock-off shades are returned,
I'll gladly return your iPod,
no questions asked
about your shopping habits."

Not surprisingly the deal never went down.

Pennsylvania Hotel

Outside this home of disparates,
in a wash of a dank afternoon
on rain slicked pavement
a blurred traffic light blinks
with smatterings of gaudy neon.

Rogues and vagrants
scurry toward
a precarious night
by a city storm drain
where trouble is flowing out
instead of down.

In a Nutshell

Urbananity

A pause in the enveloping afternoon
parched tan grass of an inner-city park
hosts a shopping cart
with bulging bags of empty bottles
and possessions from our worlds detritus
shading a napping vagrant.

Fish

White porcelain bowl
delicately painted
glossy blue fish
swimming around forever
peacefully.

Tomato Paste

Smallest potentate
in the can cupboard
weighing in at
15.6 grams
labelled with images
of abundant tastiness
red sun filled orbs
super compact
like this poem.

Lucky

Lucky urban crow
feasts on tasty
yet not so smart brains
of splayed black roadkill squirrel.

Gotta feed the kids.

Green Olives

A glass jar of green olives
succulent bulging red centres
potently waiting silently
in the counter light
saturated gems
of Spanish sunshine
in Mama's salty marinade.

The Commute

Veil of exhaustion
wraps homebound workers
in the Friday exodus.

Screams

Screams of glee
from squeaky swings
children's flying preschool.

Lobster

A six foot mannequin lobster
stands in a shoe store window
looking for eight perfect runners
to escape the awaiting pot
of boiling water.

Summer Ferry

Hot cars jostling
in the scorching sun
glinting chrome sparkles
melting bumper to bumper
in ferry line up
impatient to join the summer
and the welcoming bay beyond.

Big black pickup arrives
and blocks the view.

Travels

Map of India

Walking through the autumn cold rain,
crunching coloured leaves that have almost all fallen
in endless patterns of random deteriorating beauty,
I came to a large puddle
in the shape of a map of India.

Rain drops caused inner waves
rippling out to the coast
hemmed by a cluster of leaves
crushed along the top where the Himalayas rise
and I thought of you.
Far away caressed between
those ever warm oceans lapping the shores,
marginally cooled by mountain breezes.

You
residing in the neighbourhood of nirvana
married to a family
of Hindu Gods and Saints
alone and at one
with that abundant sea of humanity
wrapped in a hot embrace
of Mother India.

En España

Sunday fast train at 280 kph
into Sevilla warmth of 28 Celsius
through arid rolling hills
layered with centuries of conquerors history,
Romanos, Moros, Cristianos.
Over voluptuous rolling hills
vast patchwork rectangles
of tan wheat fields
next to mustard yellows
and verdant swaths of tall swaying stalks
all topped with jubilant sunflower faces,
dotted rows of pale green lace
of sun drenched wizened olive trees,
rows of Andalusian blood oranges
and topiaried grape vines.
Past clustered white Cubist
thick walled pueblos,
shaded by red clay tile roofs
homes of grand familias
each full of local characters,
faithfully anchored
by an ornate Catholic church spire.

Our train races like the heart of a speeding swallow
through heat wave mirages
viewed out the bar car window
all enjoyed with a cerveza con limón.

Koi

They appear as languid layabouts
self-centred beauties
beneath a rippling reflective surface of glass
going slowly nowhere in their soaking wet world
of Buddha like tranquility.

Waving tissue thin fins
twinkling jackets of white and orange,
nature's spotted creations like Dalmatians or Appaloosas
satiated after this mornings breakfast scuffle
and now amusingly kissing algae off slimy rocks.

Contrast here, my stress consumed life
speeding past in a flood
of an overwhelming monologue.

They don't share my anxiety of completing taxes,
venturing across a busy street
and enduring life's aggravations.

They have blind faith in Bob, the maintenance man
who doesn't speak Japanese,
but will hopefully keep their filtration pump on.

Whether captive or bored they glide safely
knowing no pencil legged heron
or a fisherman's spear
will be hovering
with a fat fish dinner in mind
of a Koi delicacy, grilled, fried or sashimied.

RVing

Right from a travelogue film;
hotel suites on wheels, customized caves,
tricked out set ups, with creature comforts
from pint sized demure to state of the art ostentatiousness.

Let the wind blow, start your big engine, relocate your home,
discover new vistas, create new neighbours.

Inhabited by a unique cast of characters, amorphous clans,
more varied than a casting director could assemble,
each with stories of their lives left behind,
lumbering like hippos along highways and backroads
returning to wandering ways.

Stylish white boxes with emblazoned logos-
Winnebago, Slumber Queen, Arctic Fox,
Odyssey Coach, Mountain Aire.
Are these names thought up
in the same marketing offices as paint names?

At the RV Park, tucked in-between trees,
out of life's busy ways
in a maze of sites by rivers and lakes,
they appear unconnected to this harried world.

At dusk these nomads
share stories and drinks around campfires,
smoking away vampire mosquitoes,
while above, a woodpecker taps out
an evening dessert of bugs
and from the neighbour's fifty-five foot Caravan Queen,
the TV light flickers through a screened window
and you can overhear a detective mumbling,
"I don't think your husband did it either, Ma'am."

Marrakesh Market

In the throngs of hustle and hassle,
like hunters, long before we see them
they see us,
smell us coming.

Hello, bonjour
good morning for you
Excuse me
Please lady come see
You too gentleman
You arrive here is good luck
I show you something
Nice colours
Pleasure for your eyes
I know your taste Madame
My pleasure talk to you
Lot of quality
Need I to explain more?
Where you from?
Montreal?
I have cousin in Montreal
Shawarma shop twelve years
Have look dis
Very nice pieces
Only hand made
I have others
You want to see different?

No walk away
I don't push
You come inside
3, 4 minutes
Just looking
You can admire
This carpet like Aladdin's
will fly home with you
chipping included
I will tempt you with tempting price
better than money in bank
How much you pay?
I make you shocking shocking price
Your wife is more Scottish
No problem
You buy for family
Take your time
You buy is better
You no buy
I shake your hand
You still my friend
Welcome very much.

Morocco

Vast flat arid desert, parched sea of sand,
stretches to the horizon,
scarred by thirsty curving vacant riverbeds.

Shifting lifting dunes
soft moving contours
fine, round rolling sand, sand, sand
then only rocks harshly wind scoured, sun scorched.

Lines of scruffy thorny grasses
twisted anorexic trees delineating underground streams
spelling life for Moroccan herds of sheep, goats
chaperoning nomads, children of the wind
riding sturdy camels and compliant donkeys.

Oasis water sources, not mirages
replete with sweet sun-drenched date palms
tasty olives, generous figs, oily almonds and juicy oranges
ancient kasbahs in transitions of ruin
a songbird's refuge.

Last year, this year, no rain, before, very little.
Once was an ocean
now majestic stratified mountains
laced with nautilus and petrified shellfish
a geologist's paradise.
Tortured switchbacks through the Atlas and Riff Mountains
gorges and valleys, prehistoric millenniums, Mesolithic
stories.

Red brick villages appear as monochromatic apparitions
rising from coloured earth,
camouflaged, visible by dark silhouette shadows
of windows and doorways
dusted with a haze of evening cooking smoke.
A nation where heat is a permanent resident
that steals away at night.

Place names; salted, citric, honey
melting Moorish tastes
Tazzarine, Tangiers, Skoura, Arfoud, Fez.

From towering ornate minarets, come supplications
resonant in harmonious dissonance for the faithful.
Prayers to Allah the Beneficent
talks with God five times a day.
Behind high walls, in cool hallowed halls
men in rows kneel bowing towards Mecca
on intricately woven carpets
women at the back
Muslims from tribes of
Ahl Serif, Beni Amir, Berber, Souss.

Ninety-nine names for the servants of God,
Abdulbaktar
Abdulmalek
Abderaman
Abdelhadi
Abdelkader
Abdelsamad
Abdelhassen
Abdelsalam
Inshallah~God Willing.

continued . . .

Men in djellabas, sitting in cafes
bittersweet mint tea, cigarettes, parched throats
stoic, opinionated, turbaned, chiseled, wizened
standing by shadowy walls, timeless statues.

Women not so visible, shrouded in veils, niqabs, burqas, hijabs
round faces, sharp Arabic tongues, darting black olive eyes
viewing a jilted type of security
shopping, then floating back home.
A peculiar role for these mothers of men.

This mystifying Moroccan life, so different, appearing exotic.
An arid balancing equation, life co-existing between
the harsh dry breath of the desert
and this people's indomitable spirit.

Season Opener March 2020

Before this Season's Opener
Covid 19 showed up.

Everything was cancelled
soccer, baseball, basketball, cricket,
FIFA, Wimbledon, the Olympics.
Around the world
east, west, north, south,
no fun and no one won.
Work, movies, concerts, exhibitions
and my favourite social dancing,
imparting a feeling of demotion, with angst in the air
even among the fortunate people of the world.

Churches, mosques and temples all closed
the Gods seemed to be on a hiatus
or else sending us a message.
An exponential globalization of
sickness, tragedy and death
half a million and counting.

Medical teams, first responders
grocery clerks and truck drivers
our heroes and heroines.

The lifestyle we knew vanished
replaced by a new age of dissonance,
a challenging adjustment
to a hugless two meter separation.
Acts of kindness entered the play
and Mother Earth
got to take big breaths of fresh air again.

Paris Brasserie

Overflowing onto the sidewalk with patrons
as colourful as a florist's storefront.
Attentive, veteran waiters
starched white aprons, vests, bow ties
attitude and gymnastic flare
carrying trays heavy with drinks.
A soundtrack of jazz classics
Vin rouge ou blanc et Gauloise Bleu.

This nationality uses their eyebrows
to say so much.
Couples socializing,
French kissing.
They smoke with laisséz faire
a sense of youthful omnipotence
strutting around in showy couture.
They've perfected the art of wearing elegant scarves
pride of the perfect man bag
and riding bicycles the wrong way
down narrow one-way streets.

They have the finesse of knowing running shoes
are for exercising only.

Tulum

Pasty white gringos and milk chocolate locals,
rest and play, under white cotton candy clouds,
sailing in the constant blue sky
above the turquoise Caribbean shore's sandy skirt.

A distant reef marks a line of white wave dashes
telling tales of pirate shipwrecks
resting silently below, full of salty tales
of fortunes plundered and lost
amongst the jewelled corals
and the darting eyes of timid techni-coloured fish.

Silent pelicans glide in tropical winds
diving, fishing below the crests
as breezes buffet, caress and bless
these ancient sun-baked shores
by this magical Mayan jungle.

Up the slope, territorial iguanas
wait for a passing gravy train
of tasty ant treats.
On the shore, the spiralling currents
collect and wash up blankets of green salad seaweed
mixed with a devastating show of our world's gift
of coloured plastic detritus,
all under the dancing shade patterns
of the rhythmical clattering palm leaves.

The waves will never stop their hypnotic crescendo
punctuated with joyful notes of children
playing until the sun melts into the sea
and mothers collect them for their pilgrimage home.

Subway

Ground out of darkness
stretched tunnel mazes
in coal black veins
comes deafening steel wheels screeching
clattering, clanking, careening
cars after cars flashing by
accelerating, braking
never sleeping
insomniac anacondas on speed
racing, rapidly, rattling, rumbling
on overburdened arterial networks
shaking pavement and foundations
heralding throngs of purposeful commuters
reloading entering, resting, leaving
safety sealed doors open
spewing out moving masses
each enclosed in their own private
earbud soothed world
cross-town, midtown, uptown
surging, pumping people
the city's blood
with every different accented language
insular moles spewing from the underworld
through turnstile mouse traps
back up into the light
funnelling into steel and glass towers
that mushroom above ground.

Sheepish

On a holiday in Ireland we rented a car,
driving on the left side of the road
five speed stick shift on the right
narrow twisty roads
lined with abundant ivy and ferns hiding rock walls,
excellent for smashing off your side view mirror.

The agency had included a navigation system
we named Phyllis,
who guided us through the hills and dales
and umpteen shades of green.

She was as knowledgeable as any local
until she had us turn down a farmer's lane
then onto a track, "Turn left here, turn left here,"
into a field full of woolly sheep.

They all stopped eating; looking up, barely astonished
muttering amongst themselves,
"Damn, farmer Heaney forgot to close the gate again,"
they bleated with a strong Irish brogue.
"Can we help you please, you seem to be lost."
"This isn't the sweater department."
"We're too old to be made into lamb chops."

After waving and making some lame baaahhh imitations
we asked Phyllis to take a tea break
reversed out of the muddy field
and got back on the road.

We consulted a wrinkled old map
without fear of driving off the edge of the earth
into one of its torn folded corners.

Reappearance

When I return home in a daze
exchanging realities from being far away
adjusting time zones,
it's always a big stretch to fit into
what I tell myself are my old clothes,
trying them on each day
with an element of uncertainty.
Where is my "Belonging" T-shirt?

Regrettably I extricated myself,
from an inspiring cultural perspective
varieties of characters, costumes and cuisines
the intoxicating foreign language soundtrack
relished with all my senses,
being comfortable with sometimes being uncomfortable
in a foreign spider web of beauty and wonder.

I'm home now, the bubble has burst.
Do I really live here under this monotonous dank grey sky?
Or was that sun-drenched affair
that foreign exotic kiss, true love?

Where do I really belong?
Which puzzle piece is the right fit?
Should I escape to a warm foreign land
and always be from away?
Could I afford the price of change
an immigrant must pay?
Or should I look closer in my mirror
and see that this hometown
looks the best on me.

Family and Friends

Hey Sweetpea

Let's see what Sally says about that
She's coming over soon
and she always has lots to say,
wafting in here with her weekend smile
sweet as sun-ripened fruit.

She's not yet discovered its secret
where it hides
or how to hold onto it
when the going gets rough.

Yesterday, she told me
how she loved dancing with the Texans
their stomping boots stirring a haze of dust
in the coloured blinking stage lights
such gentlemen buying her shots and chasers
rustling brouhaha at the bar,
those boys, some more complicated than others.

She's had some close calls
but never with the law, Thank God.

Some things she's told me, some things she hasn't
some things she did, some things she didn't.

With the sun setting into another night,
looking in her closet, worrying about what to wear.
smiling, she remembers her mom saying
"as you grow older Sweetpea,
each decade brings a gift
of being a new you."

Heather

A ring came on
a ring came off.
I learned a lot
about human nature.

The swing of love and separation
the havoc of a starter marriage,
beginning with love forever,
planting our dreams
in a coloured perennial garden
perishing after 6 years.

With the energy of our 30s
an old house restoration
bee keeping
wind surfing
in the crazy 80s.

Expo exploded,
we had a situation,
she chose polygamy
a cruel obsession
too big for our waterbed.
Corrosive, flammable, explosive.

It took a year
to turn my back
and cross the bridge
encasing my heart
in a concrete bunker.

Birthday Balloons

Oh, look what arrived today!
Bright primaries, turquoises and mauves,
a universal symbol of fun
bopping from luminous ribbons
foretelling a grand celebration.

Along with them came cards of effusive wishes
for a new year full of happiness,
though we all know there'll be
laughter and tears
accomplishments and failures.

They're seamlessly smooth
contrasting my accumulated crow's feet,
another year's depreciation
like an uninvited visitor staring at me in the mirror
who at times, I'd rather not acknowledge.

When the party's over
if you aren't worried about brain cells
inhaling the helium happy gas
reawakens the youngster inside of you.

Over the passing years
I've seen lonesome escapees
waywardly hanging in trees like deflated condoms.
Recently, after passing a special decade
one glided like a cat from room to room
in the day's summer breezes.

Whole years pass with
gifts of innumerable experiences.
On the outside, older yes
a little rust on this model
but not on the inside.

Lists

I love my habit of making lists of things-to-do,
written on small squares of cut up paper,
a habit adjacent to an addiction:

- weekend errands to run
- groceries
- appointments
- a Honey-do list
- special tunes I've heard
- books and movies to read and see
- tools I've lent to friends
- time on the couch, not on any list.

After completing each
they get scribbled out and a satisfying check mark.

I have language lists of fascinating words
heard, written or read
nouns, verbs, concepts, percepts,
ordinary yet distinct,
twists of phrases, colloquialisms
for speaking, writing and singing.

Some I've lost, as I don't have a list of where I put my lists
and my wife regards them as litter.

Really they are like ripe autumn apples picked from
neighbouring trees
waiting their turn in the cold cellar
before reappearing in our kitchen
with ingredients from my baking list
to be cooked into a pie, cobbler or crisp
served up warmly with vanilla ice cream
all in a scrumptious poem.

August 16th

One day defined in the smoke of history,
228th day of the Gregorian calendar
229th in leap years, (if you're keeping count)
Astrologically – Leo, the best sign of twelve.

I've had so many days celebrating my specialness,
cards both tender and curiously cynical
about that ever increasing number
spaced between years of cloudy doubt.
Yes, there have been presents
and the fortunate presence of friends.

Many times that song has been sung
my name scrolled on a chocolate cake.
Years of turning the lights on in the morning and off at night.

Up until 21, I wanted to be a year older, then I didn't.
My first ten were innocent, the teens fermented, twenties
spent travelling, thirties art school and starter marriage.
forties divorced and recovery, fifties remarried and
renovating sixties plain intimidating.

On this day, notables were born:
Pete Best, The Beatles' original drummer – 1962
Bill Evans, American jazz pianist – 1929
Madonna, never invited me to her birthday parties – 1957.
I'd like to dance with her, she must be pretty good.

And on this day, others have died:
Elvis Presley, on a hot August day at 42
Lawrence of Arabia, on a motorcycle – 46
Aretha Franklin - Queen of Soul – 76
Noah, old age – 950

Born the same year, with a different life path:
Stevie Wonder, Arianna Huffington, Bill Murray
Bruce "The Boss" Springsteen.
None the happier
I've learned that happiness only goes as high as 10.

The sand pours through my hourglass.
I have pride in my life of accumulated experience
with all these large decades stacking up.
I'm a day closer to sliding off the cliff
into the unknown mist.

Buttons

We have a friend
from Florida
married to its sunshine
and a lovely wife.

He has buttons made
with faces of faraway friends
who have passed away,
sporting them over his big heart
especially on days
when he misses them the most.

They speak of the poems of their lives
favourite times remembered
streams followed
valleys spanned
oceans navigated
friends of the heart.

With spirits rejoined
their energy lives on again
revolving around the day's events
discussing warm fields of memories
the precious hold of great loves
shared together.

Maria

We had private conversations
in a unique language without words,
sharing great understandings
disregarding gaps we couldn't cross
after your stroke of bad luck at two years old.

So wonderfully affectionate
beautiful with bangs.

Our after- school adventures,
joyfully playing crawling tag
around the dining room table
up and down the stairs
calluses on our knees.

With my other sis we helped you practice walking
on a hallway ballet bar
and on steel parallel bars in the back yard
that Dad had made.
We covered them with blankets for a playhouse
under the grace of our cherry tree.

Sis and I weren't included in conversations
about the institution which became your home at 14.
You in your wheelchair disappeared
into a secret world behind stark walls
with echoing halls of misunderstanding
because Mom was dying
and couldn't cope anymore.

Christina Lake

I shared fourteen joyous summers playing at Jericho Beach
digging impossibly deep sand pits
with my two sisters, Carol and Maria,
and finding from the tide, a perfect pole
that we draped with a blanket Mom let us use
to shelter in the shade of our perfect world.

After school when the loud teenagers arrived,
we helped Maria walk back to our Sunbeam Hillman
so mom could make dinner and have it on the table at six.

For my 15th summer
Dad talked with the neighbours, the Coopers.
Off I went to Christina Lake
with my new turquoise surfboard
that dad had patiently taught me to build
on the ping pong table in the basement
while upstairs, Carol was learning from mom how to cook
as she lay in bed dying.

I prayed to Jesus to take Dad instead
I loved Mom more
Hope did not trump reality.

The Coopers catered fun,
swimming and picnicking in the sun.
On dark waters we sang.
"Come on Sweetpea, come on and dance with me."
And with teenage wildness
we pushed a rusted Austin across a grassy field, over the cliff
to plunge cinematically into the lake's depths.

Much of the time, in shorts and T-shirt,
I sat alone, hidden among the cool speechless trees
inside myself, within a vast void
in a silent loss deeper than the lake
rippling with memories, drowning in an uncertain future
struggling with what should not have been,
life without my mother's magnanimous heart
no longer wrapping a warm blanket around our family.

Michael Kerry

High school buddies
graduated then hatched a trip,
to hitchhike away from home across this vast country.
Rolling across the prairies with music,
The Beatles, Dylan and Jimi,
waking in Leonard's Montreal,
hopping a passenger freighter
for a rough November Atlantic crossing.

Scotland, Britain in a cold VW van
then inside a tin can Citroen
winding in a hash haze through France, Italy,
hiking around Crete,
devouring tomatoes, cucumbers and halva,
wintering in the caves of Matala with Joni
then a helter-skelter saga from Istanbul
with British hippies in a bread van
dressed in foolishness and fearlessness,
palpable uncertainty and diarrhea.
Transitioning across exotic
tortuous mountains and vast monochrome deserts
feeling omnipotent without a compass.

Turkey, Iran, Afghanistan, Pakistan
home on the road, getting lost and found with sun-baked
stoners and drug dealers
dabbling in contraband shipping.

Melting into the presence
of Mother India's embrace and abundance
amid spiced, sweltering tumultuous millions
tattooed brothers at a Shiva festival
a Taj Mahal acid trip
sharing blazing chillums with sadhus.
So many adventures risked and survived
for the brave and the crazy like us.

When our paths forked
I never imagined it was a final goodbye.

I rested at an ashram
on the Arabian Ocean coast
carrying water, chopping wood,
creativity and peace,
a blend of Hinduism and Buddhism
a type of fathomable spirituality.

You returned to the allure of the road,
disregarding vulnerability
disappearing forever
in the shadowy alleys
of Bombay's opioid veins.

Nearly Drowned

Wasn't just anywhere where it happened,
it was on the banks of the Yukon river
way up north in Dawson City
at the Klondike Fine Malt Society's monthly event.

The experienced imbibers were joyously and conscientiously
blind tasting eight varieties concealed in brown paper bags.
Whoever identified which was which
would win a bottle of Lagavulin scotch.

Comparative discussions were wildly flying about.
Laughter, biases and conclusions
were being pounded on the kitchen table
as they marked their tasting charts
for smokiness, peatiness and smoothness
when a scream came from the bathroom.

Lulu had dropped her cell in the toilet.
She said, when backing up it just slipped
out of the back pocket of her new Carhart jeans.
An honest mistake but with all the shenanigans going on
what actually happened is another story.

Good luck was proffered and remedies
of CPR in the microwave
as the plastered members stumbled out
into minus 30 flurries.

Next morning when she sobered up
resuscitation in a bowl of dry rice
kept it from dying,
carrying it on for a good life
for another five years.

Mike Frastacki's Solo Road

Yesterday, I happened
to walk down the road
where you used to live.
Tears after you left
have been washed away by the rain.

You criss-crossed the globe alone
trekking across the spines
of Tajikistan and Uzbekistan,
descending into Allah's tortured Afghanistan
to a sun-kilned valley of Nahrin
with one God for all these lawless tribes.

Your conviction of building a school
and playground for 300 eager urchins
yearning to learn and to play
amongst the lingering shrapnel of wars.

When the dust had settled
and the bullet's blast fell silent,
you joined the departed there
but your dreams aren't buried.
They bloom in that harshness
on the opposite side of this unsettled globe.

Murmuring

Beauty tragedy mystery,
lives wrapped in tissue paper skins
murmuring palliative hallways
mumbled memories of lives lived and loved.

Rough potholed roads, rocks, ravines.
Patients searching for glimpses of a healthy oasis
slow motion downhill
hoping for a U turn not an exit sign
extended travel visa for this world denied.

Innocent souls resting in good hands
chaperoned by nurses, uniformed in compassion
dispensing one more pain placating pill
or a morphine poppy drip.

Days melting too quickly between unconscious nights,
finite days captured by a destiny of illness
in the not-getting-better ward.
Preparing to meet The Maker.

Time here shrinking for bewildered shufflers
in hospital socks with IV pole companions
beds of full lives with hazy futures
wistfully reaching an expiry date
accepting four syllable ailments.

Previously automatic body parts ceasing
non-cooperating vital organs,
unscripted stage four qualifiers,
the lottery of anatomical diseases
vanquishing the logic of medicine.

A premature game changer,
caught in a crease of fortune,
society's contributors not wanting
to depart to the other side.
Which side is better?

Different pasts, similar dissolutions
slipping into dreams of beatitude
sifting the dust of favourite memories,
unique songs of life fading to their last sonorous bars.

Good souls alone, sleep soundly tonight
until the last breath
when the fickle finger of fate scrolls
through the favourite scenes to The End,
leaving behind, the curse of sorrow.

Love never dies
though loved ones leave.

Unfortunately

I count on more than two hands
this list, grown to a heavy baker's dozen
of those now pushing up daises
leaving me left alone with a bus full of memories
and my feelings separated only
by a thin shoe sole protection
from our world's harshness.

Losing friends,
lost richness of inconceivable value.
It wasn't their idea to leave,
some by choice, others by lottery.

Not in chronological order
Tanya, diabetes complications
Chris, took his life
Richard, a cancer casualty
Michael K, disappeared in the alleys of Bombay,
Michael F, murdered in the mountains of Afghanistan,
Diane, my favourite former girl friend
Maureen, my wife's sister
Gerald, gifted me the inspiration to write poetry
Cecile, left three kids and her man behind
David, Charles and Brian, three top drawer carpenters
Brian, a defunct heart pump,
Danny, flipped his ATV
David, a Covid victim.
Gunther, the scourge of ALS.
Departing too early
I miss them in more ways than I can say,
I didn't get to say goodbye to most.
We shared such good stories
created friendships now finished
better than any characters in my favourite novels
now carefully reserved on a haloed bookshelf
in the warm inner home of my heart.

Shyness

To traverse life's difficulties, on occasion,
I talk to a counsellor.
Once, while discussing dealing with a maniac boss
I noticed a book on shyness
purporting in bold coloured type
Living Fully with Shyness and Social Anxiety
I made a note to buy it.

Months later, on a hot summer afternoon
I parked my wife at a coffee shop along Broadway
then walked a few blocks
to Odin's Metaphysical and Self Help Bookstore.
Entering the silence, I revealed my note to the attendant
who found the book hidden at the back of the store
on the bottom shelf.

Walking back along the baking sidewalk
at a busy intersection, edging up to the crosswalk
was the broad face of an express B Line accordion bus
with my good buddy Neil sitting at the wheel.
He opened the door and I hopped on.

We chatted speedily for some kilometres
then I announced to his passengers
that today was their driver's birthday
which I knew it wasn't.

Suddenly remembering my wife back in the coffee shop
I hopped off at the next stop.
Later, he told me they'd all sung him Happy Birthday.

Questioning my shyness,
I gave the book to the Sally Ann
and changed jobs.

Teenage Years

Four decades ago my teenage eyes opened
in the smoke of a Cold War world.
The 60s spread out a divergent travesty.

On walks home from high school
I sifted through a vague global understanding
mixed with the six o'clock news
explosions in Vietnam
rumblings across our neighbour's border
felt through our home,
festering a generational battle of wills.
Signals crossed with seeds of dis-adoption
opposing ideologies.
Flower power versus a corporate war machine.

Mom died in June the night before my electrical exam,
AC and DC currents short circuited our family's
connectedness
my conversations with Dad crashed like crushed ice
freezing into a glacier, neither being able to thaw.
He saw my opinions from a middle-class upbringing
as rebellious antipathy,
hindsight says it was adolescent presumptuous omnipotence.

Summer of love bloomed.
Taking Dad's business acumen,
I segued into faltering entrepreneurship,
Mexican sweet red wine cured pot; $200 a kilo
dealing nickel bags on 4th to pay my first digs' rent
keeping stoned with friends as often as possible.

I walked an undefined road looking for meaning,
delicate, awkward, naive, curious
feeling life had thrown me questionable cards.

After one year of college, at 19
with youthful presumptions
I hitchhiked through the Rockies
blown rudderless across the vast prairies to Montreal
boarded a trans-Atlantic freighter
a Europe tour, overland to India
sketching a saga, searching for a why
and any form of nurture.

Sweet Jesus
- Inspired by John Prine - The Missing Years

I love carpentry.
For years, it paid my double digit mortgage
on the east side of town.
Once, at a Union meeting
when the brass wouldn't give us a raise
Bob stormed out shouting
"For God's sake, Jesus was a carpenter."

As a teen, His Virgin Mother Mary had sent the lad out
to work with his step-dad Joseph, a woodworker.
His real Dad was away, working on bigger stuff,
and not revealing what was in store.

In my Sunday school classroom there was a painting of Jesus
under the shade of an olive tree, planing a board
as I've done, making a pile of curly shavings under a
cedar tree.
Another painting depicted Him
returning from a camping trip in the desert
with village kids clustering around His dusty sandals
outstretched palms, speaking of love and luminous truths.

In the Good Book, it isn't written
about His woodworking skills.
Fortunately, the gig wasn't a good fit
and changing careers became a blessing.
So he got busy meeting guys in the smelly fish business
hanging with some good shepherds
and growing a taste for red wine cultivars.

Every Sunday morning, I squirmed on a hard pew bench
in itchy wool flannel pants Mom had dressed me in
while I dreamed of playing outside in shorts.

During that hour off on Sunday
Mom and my sis, Maria,
(who couldn't walk nor talk), had one on one time.

Mom, being a lapsed Catholic
knew that the Good Lord
wouldn't be creating any miracles for her
as He was off closing and opening doors for other folk.

What Are The Chances

I'm not a betting guy, it's not immoral.
I like watching sports, mostly rooting for the underdog
but not sports betting.
Buying lottery tickets may spur one's imagination of
'what if'
but they always make me feel like a loser.
I walk past the bingo hall with an ounce of curiosity
preferring to ante up at the pub down the block
where a beer with a friend always pays off big.

It is not in me to consider skydiving
leaving terra firma, jumping out at 10,000 feet
above some farmer's field, presumably without cows
with instructions on how to roll.
Come on please,
I'm the type who gravitates to comfy chairs.
a cup of tea and a good book.

With love and luck
I've had an array of queen cards played
some have dealt me rejection
others, regrettably I've failed to send thank you cards to.
Flowers for my Sweetheart are a sure bet
and dancing lessons have proven beneficial.

My old Magic 8 Ball was truthful to a point,
wishbone pulls have had favourable outcomes
and I'd like to address whoever writes those fortune cookies
topping off the Chinese take-out;
you ancient sage, sitting cross legged
twirling your sparse crinkly beard
bamboo brush scripting charcoal on rice paper.

I fall on my knees to your wit, predictions of the future
with their accuracy, humour and no guarantees.

Thank you for trying so hard to line up what may come.
To be honest
I admit trying to peek over your shoulder occasionally
to see how my tomorrows may unfold.

The Jones

The Jones (not their real name) are an interesting couple
a conjoining of opposites, one might say.

Two compositions of uniqueness
woven together with the intricacies of a Persian carpet.

They have a special thing going
magic you know, which can't be bought or sold.

She loves to drink strong coffee in the morning
He drinks tea all day, calling it his happy juice.

They are cat people now
although both have had numerous dogs.

He has nightmares of claustrophobia
she, of her son having an accident.

Her son brings brightness and caring
For him he adds double gain.

From Lady Luck and hard work
(I'm not sure in which order)
they have every convenience
stove and fridge, dishwasher, washer/dryer.

She loves babies more than apple pie and whipping cream
He finds peace creating things from wood and clay.

Sometimes when he says white
she says black, of which she has a lot in her wardrobe.

After dinner she likes watching detective series.
By teeth brushing time, he wants to know if the killer
was caught.

They lather over any cracks of disagreements
with an immense love they share for each other.

They've collected more beautiful artwork
than they can fit on their bungalow walls.

Both love listening to all types of music
but neither can comprehend rap.

Dad

A large man but not a big talker
hair cut as crisp as toast
our bread winning pillar
confident, quiet, stern, steady
loving in his own way
bravely flew in the RCAF through WW 2.

He fixed things, from the weekend honey-do list
on the back kitchen porch
on a cool summer morning
he expertly and casually repaired Mom's clothespins
I was in awe, now I fix things.

He'd walk past the raspberry patch to the garage
cleaning ear wax with his car keys
a pressure relief valve that freed him
until the family caught up
and piled into his warmed up Studebaker.

At the summer exhibition,
in matching Hawaiian shirts and shorts Mom had sewn,
on a perfect cotton candy day by the merry go round,
he paid a mysterious man 10 cents to guess my age
Five!
How does he do that Daddy?

Working for approval
and with his intermittent patience
he left me alone to dust off, sand and varnish
a cedar 14 foot sailboat, Hot Rum,
his pride from before his marriage to Mom
had cancelled further sailings.

Home everyday from the office for lunch
in our kitchen nook.
After doctoring up the city's bus system
to fit its growing needs,
he'd sip a glass or two of sherry at five to six
relaxing with the evening paper,

He showed me it's OK for strong men to cry
a good father of us three kids
too soon in mid-life a single parent.

With decades of well washed memories
I've learned so much
in our years together and apart.
We travelled far and since his death,
I have grown only closer.

I don't remember many specifics
but I'm still a sum of lessons learned
from my ponderous father figure.

My Wife's Sisters

I won the sister-in-law lottery.
Marie Bernadette
Louise Antoinette
Maureen Yvonne
Grace Marcella
Corinne Lucille.
Dramatic queens
large in infectious spirit
eccentrics, zingers in their own special way
all enjoyable as smooth red wine
powder keg beauties
gentle and feisty as a cat
not as different as black and white
let's say Irish green and cranberry red.
Loving Moms
wizard cooks
wild blueberry pickers
ocean and lobster lovers
stable in a storm
enthusiastic with a capital E
confident and caring to a fault
trustworthy and tolerant to a T
imbibers in the cups
who fill a kitchen party with laughter
and make you forget the winter's cold.
Scrabble addicts
with a special way to say their Rs
some good Nova Scotian story tellers
the best in Canada.

Living apart, connected in heart
and "Lord tunderin' Jesus"
I wouldn't trade any
for my number one squeeze
Patricia Anne.

South Carolina

What was the name of your boyfriend
not the tightrope walker, before him
the blue grass one from South Carolina
rhythmic banjo and synchronized beard
wailing Avett Brothers' love lyrics
two, three, four harmonies.
Too long in the years for your spirit.

As a pair you'd paddled far
along strings of rivers in Northern Ontario
crashing white waters of the
Missinaibi, Noire, Pettawawa
bugs and back woods stories
sung into a brief history
running its course to the Hudson's Bay.
Two characters, from two oceans apart
hopeful love songs, funny looks,
vaporizing under a moon
languidly lying upside down.

You say you might never see him again,
no more pickup trucks, no regrets
changed ways written in a high cold spray
paddling watery swirls into an eddying song,
applause not needed.

Around The House

Our Clothesline

It's in our side yard
stretched taut and thin
on squeaky pulleys
from porch to post.

In the warm morning out from the basket
pinned up in order with weathered wooden pegs
garlands of floral sheets
transforming into full billowing sails blowing
in the summer wind.

Towels, jeans, shirts, t-shirts, shorts, dresses,
an apron, socks and undies
dangling randomly in a jazzy arrangement
waving to the neighbours
and their dancing shadows
in a fresh-air embrace.

Before the evening dew
all neatly folded
back in the basket.

Bowls

Once was part of a tree,
curious wooden gnarl
saltwater scrubbed
tide and wind blown
beached at high tide
crab hiding shelter
sniffed at by dogs
picked up by a carver
transformed into a unique bowl
holding precious ocean stones
keys, a lock of hair.

Ants

Spring appeared around the corner quickly,
like a baby lamb jumping among the daffodils,
the birds and the bees zooming by.

Ants arrived too,
evolving from the Cretaceous Period
approximately 66 million years ago.
This morning, out from the hallways
of their dark apartment,
they drew skittish lines
of exploratory expeditions across our kitchen floor
gleaning vital nutrients, carrying home morsels
from yesterday's bread making endeavour.
Some cultures eat them fried or dipped in chocolate,
apparently, a crunchy delicacy
but not on my menu.

These six articulate legged miniature creations
determined, communicative, problem solving
super organisms operating as a unified entity
clear divisions of labour between queens, reproductive males
drones and soldiers supporting a healthy home for their
colony.
Inspirational parallels for our own human society.

Dammit,
out front they're even chewing up a crack in the sidewalk.
In this neck of the woods, anteaters or aardvarks
don't appear from the local exterminator's van
and I couldn't imagine
these new housemates parading around,
so on an expedition to the hardware store
I bought some sodium tetraborate decahydrate - Borax.

They found it tasty, dutifully carrying it home
affecting their metabolism, abrasing their exoskeleton
and just like the Jonestown mass murder suicide
they all died
until a week later, when their relatives arrived.

Her Jewellery Organizer

My wife's jewellery lives
dangling on the back
of our bathroom door.
Sparkling behind clear plastic crinkled pockets
displayed in a black mini dress silhouette
with a scoop neckline
sewn three compartments across
twelve down.

She chooses each day
necklaces with gems and suns
filigree hearts, beads and spangles
silver hoops, brooches, charms, rings
sparkling pendants pins and pearls.
One for every outfit
supplementing her beauty
suitable adornment for a Goddess.

Folding Laundry

As for most,
some days are better than others.
There's sunny blue sky
then others are washed in inky darkness.

The clothes hamper fills like an abstract hourglass.
On laundry day I revel in folding
the softness into orderly piles
while the day's worst stories unfold
in the flickering light of the 10 o'clock news.

Happy Shoes

Can shoes walk you to happiness?

Last night, I carried my black loafers
big holes in the soles, now lifeless
like a dead pooch in my arms
out to the garbage,
along with an evening's empty bottle of red.
If I was starring in a movie, it would have been raining.

It felt like shooting my old, devoted hound.
Who would want to do that?
Even my cobbler had given them the thumbs down.
This side of the world
no one wants this old pair.

Tomorrow, Alice in an Econo van
will collect bottles from the alley
helping her daughter through university
graduating with a microbiology degree,
or the lady from the corner house
will retrieve them to help save African elephants.

That shoe salesman had been right
about their good fit.
They'd waltzed me down a thousand roads
seeing me through good and bad times
with flying colours.

Patio Chairs

Exposed and silently waiting
designed for comfort,
wicker, wood, webbed, plastic, aluminum
splashes of colour to match your outdoor decor.

Some are accompanied by a bored bundled umbrella
and a lonely chaise lounge languishing with a pining heart
on that perfect dappled sunlit patio
in a summer that will vanish all too soon.

Originally you deservedly purchased them,
from that hard earned paycheck,
somewhere to sit, contemplate your future,
unwind with a beer, a book or just nap.

For another day, they lay fading all by themselves,
lonesome like an abandoned hound dog,
patiently awaiting their owner's butts,
(impartial to large or small)
to be placed mercifully on their soft contours.

Come on you lucky ones,
people those chairs, soak it up,
start a club with a code of rules to relax more
cue up that soft mood music and sink
into your unused icons of privilege.

After all,
on the other side of our world,
millions are content.
to sit cross legged
on the hard ground.

Illustrious Characters

In a writing workshop, we received a prompt
to write about three significant people in our lives.

While others waxed on about the likes of Mandela,
Mahatma and King,
or Mom, Dad and the special Aunt,
for me, four others came to mind.

I guess from my colonial ancestry
and having hired help about the house,
I chose to write about servants in our employ.

Of their varied capacities and nationalities,
firstly comes Abdul, our houseboy for interior chores.
He makes the morning coffee for the Missus,
laundries and washes up what our chef refuses to do.

Gaston is the chef; he turns on his tunes and with a glass
of red,
cooks three to four course dinners,
providing sommelier services and creating bi-weekly desserts
as our midriffs can attest to.

Juan Garcia Rodriguez Sancha is our gardener,
maintaining the lawn, plantings, hedge trimming, autumn
leaves
and of course, Canadian snow shovelling
In all seasons, attempting to keep up with the neighbours.

Jarvis is our always prompt yet-aging chauffeur,
graciously accepting occasional backseat drivers.
He has an excellent driving record,
save for a few weeks when he was seeing double.

As for the help it provides
and the appearance of privilege,
it takes a great deal of managing varied personalities.

I believe they are generally a happy lot,
the pay is good, I think
and they get days off for religious holidays.

Abdul goes to his mosque every Friday.
He says he prays for us.
Juan Garcia Rodriguez Sancha disappears on Sundays
as well as all Catholic Saint Days.
Gaston is a Christian Scientist, don't get me started
and Jarvis, he is an agnostic, Thank God

If a girl can dream, so can a guy.
Who says kids are the only ones with imaginary friends?

The Road

Tow Truck Drivers

Big burly buddies polish their sunlit chrome
brightly coloured, replete with menacing chains
Herculean capacity from 5 to10 tons
and the miracle of hydraulics
hovering over 4 bad ass back tires.

A snarly bullshitting tribe
those dam jerks, polishing their rigs
waiting for the 3pm parking restriction to strike,
out like hornets from the hive
disappearing into the commuting thoroughfares
decongesting rush hour arteries
heroically extracting commuter crashes.

Rapidly reappearing, strobing orange lights
cars hooked with alarms screaming
dangling from front or back on a hefty steel crucifix
impartial to all makes and sizes, rich and poor
efficiently dropped in the urban lot
they race back out
voracious sharks for another catch.

A little later, from taxis
spew sad sack citizens,
a pissed-off line forms
up the short wooden stairs
of the trailer in the centre,
guilty as charged.

Business suits with briefcases
moms with toddlers
tradesmen with a beef
wallets in hand
impatient and exasperated
a lesson learned, perhaps.
They tap their plastic
some with supplemental blasphemies
behind the grill, the clerk has heard it all.

They retrieve their cars
their loves,
buckling up their emotions
returning to delayed plans
in a traffic choked city.

Bus Shelter

One November Saturday,
Dad hammered it together
with hope and old barn boards
while us kids played in the first snow.

Mom dressed us warmly
and on early mornings chased us
with book bags and lunches
past our cavalcade of pines
above the mighty Fraser
to wait sheltered for smiley Stan's
rumbling yellow school bus.

It stood so many years
faithful like a German Shepherd
through harsh winter tempests
chafed and baked dry by summer's heat.

Now it sadly leans saluting us
in suspended tension of decomposition
moss covered, silent, lonely
wind scoured cedar.

On route 12 traffic races on
the river and life flows by.

With an education we grew up fast.
Years later a Greyhound bus stopped
transporting us far from
Dad's roadside bus shelter.

Millennial

Tight jeans
black leather jacket
rainbow reflective shades
puffing vapour clouds
cool as a cucumber
beard and ear buds
linked to social media angst
slouching on grafittied bus bench
tapping red runners
on wet grey sidewalk
with patterned spots
of chewing gum Pointillism
waiting for his squeeze
thinking about a bunch of different stuff
oblivious of his uncharted future.

"F"

Scanning through the dictionary today
Canadian Oxford,
I turned to the first page of F's
- sixth letter of the alphabet, a consonant
- a fine moderately soft pencil lead
- music: fourth note of the diatonic scale
- device: printer's type for reproducing the letter f or F.

Abbreviations
- grammar: feminine
- temperature: fahrenheit
- physics: force
- metallurgy: fine
- music: forte
- math: function, (I didn't do well in that)
- academic: lowest category or mark.
Ms. Schooley gave me one of these for English Lit 12
never graduated, no graduation ceremony.

Because, while studying the clouds out the window
I couldn't understand her lessons of Canterbury Tales.
ADHD hadn't been recognized.
Paradoxically, a year later
I bumped on the floor of a hippy bread van
through Turkey, Iran, Afghanistan, Pakistan,
a pilgrimage to India
with 12 characters from Chaucer's Britain.

So, for a mark
- F means failure
- Who wants to admit to such an event occurring in their life?
- However, it has often been admitted, it is a precursor to success.

FA comes next,
- fine arts
- football association
- slang, fuck all, meaning nothing

Few have said, English is an easy language to learn.

Cardboard

Once stood a tall proud tree
sheltered among a forest of friends
green, breathing, bathed by rains.
Chainsaws roared,
forests dragged, trucked, pulverized, contorted
spewed into flattened cardboard
tenacious corrugated wafers
destined for a box factory.

Engineered durable packaging
hand holds, vent cut-outs, barcoded
bold graphics of fields and orchards bragging freshness.

Shipped to verdant fields
where imported itinerants Juan y Clarita
sunrise to sundown
pick and place with care, vegetables and fruits
from dusty baked rows into mountainous stacked boxes
onto a weathered flatbed, 6 high, 10 across
trucked along arteries to our urban grocery stores
then emptied and left flattened in the lane.

Bob, who'd never really fitted in
had made some bad choices
released last week, broken, friendless,
retrieved some cardboard depicting fields of plenty.
Thin, comforting, disposable
a homeless corrugated mattress
layered below an empty stomach
curled up in a sheltering doorway.

Next morning, while warming at Timmy's
a cold autumn tempest blew his bed to the middle of
Broadway.
A day of rain, cars, buses, trucks
pulverizing it to a soggy unrecognizable mush.

Tandem Exuberance

Two youthful women
laughing, riding on a bicycle
gleefully swerving,
one on the seat
arms outstretched
her fingers flying like wing tips
dancing with the wind
floating with delight
barely balancing
in the glowing summer air,
the other peddling madly, madly
along a pebbly summer path
inspiring joy
lacing together
an afternoon of exuberance.

Getting there
is the best part.

VW Bug

For all his gaseous atrocities
and his affinity for blond, blue-eyed men
Der Fürer left us some signature gifts.
His insidious moustache, a pasty comb over,
the autobahn and ingeniously
the distinctively purring air-cooled VW
and its factories.

Of the millions that rolled out
after the stigmatic war cloud blew away
a father of a kid in our Cubs' troop bought a blue one,
saying he loved their simple engineering
rear engine and stick shift,
parking it in his driveway
on tires made of real rubber.

After our bottle drives, he'd take us all for ice cream.
When the circus came to town
he had this crazy idea and we all crammed in.
It sputtered, jolted and bumped into the Big Top.
The ringmaster in a booming voice announced
How many could be in there?

We un-contorted ourselves
and out we came
from our German sardine can
straightening our green caps
and crumpled uniforms
10, 11, 12,
18, 19, 20,
23, 24, 25.
The crowd went wild.

In single file we marched off.
The circus elephant appeared
and with his wondrous trunk
pushed the little bug out.

City Buses

Back and forth they go.
The epitome of capacity and efficiency,
the city roar and fragrance of exhaling diesel,
whirring trolleys full
with an amazing jumble of characters
speaking every tongue imaginable
going to work, appointments
classes or shopping.

Back and forth.
Sit or stand up and hold on
cell phone junkies, tabloid readers, thinkers, dozers
baby carriage chaperones with their princes and princesses
wheelchair champions making it out for an excursion
cyclists hitching a ride
homeless keeping warm and dry.
Relax, let someone else do the driving.

Back and forth,
Cool caffeinated drivers
with hair-trigger feet
watching for open spaces, braking reds
toiling full up another Vancouver hill
with the relentless strength of a stubborn Greek donkey
shunting through rush hour on crowded day shifts
and racing through long empty nights.

Back and forth.
Multiple LEDs flash, changing signals
shiny advertising panels dusted with a brush of city grime
getting riders to their destination
barrelling down the open curb lane
like a hockey forward along the boards
to the next bus stop goal
steel clad brakes stopping like a loaded coal train.

Back and forth.
Yield, make space
watch out for the Express
double accordion, triple axle
Yeah, I'm coming through.
fuck you, yeah, I'm taking up two lanes
fully loaded with a hundred and ten.
We've got somewhere to go.

Back and forth.
With mostly straight-faced tired faces
private and urban
others with a smile to share
and a thank you called out
as they push out the exit door.

Highway Shrine

I know of a few places
along the highway
where screaming sirens came.

Today there stands alone
a homemade wooden cross
rapidly passed by thousands.

Who notices
where this deadly crash was born?

A shrine adorned once with fresh bouquets,
now dispersed by the seasons.
Faded plastic flowers
freshened annually on that date,
with cherished mementos
from friends and family.

A mother, a father, siblings,
all left behind
inestimably missed.

Accident, error or an intrusive fickle finger of fate
he, she or they, once very alive
singing with the car radio
in a deadly driving machine
a ton of steel, plastic, gasoline
a sudden chaotic crash,
life driven away,
all swept up now.

I didn't know them
but they were part of our city,
a little like me, perhaps a little like you,
now peacefully resting in solitude
preciously living on
in a gilded frame
on the family mantelpiece
where love has not died.

From The Bedroom

Early Morning

Early caressing
summer breeze
enters the bedroom window,
lovers' hearts resting now
wrapped in their heat
under a soft sheet of passion.

Outside
sunlight slants slender rays
through the giant green forest.

The neighbours arrive
unfurling the early morning
from an ancient cedar treetop
a commuting murder of crows.

What's up?
Tribal morning mighty gossip
a social media ruckus cawing across the airwaves
exuberantly discussing today's dining prospects,
starters, entrées, desserts, in any order,
bragging how quick their kids are growing,
how smart they are
and they're enjoying flying so much,
sharing evocative travel tales
of adventures and affections.

Insomniac

While brushing my teeth last night,
I recalled listening to the morning's talk show.

The interviewer asked the guest psychologist
about sleeping habits.

She said, in long term marriages
which hold a strong flame of romanticism,
she knew for a fact
that many couples sleep apart.

With this information I sank into my pillow
and pulled up my blankets
expecting a deep sleep
and sweet dreams.

Unbeknownst to me,
I was snoring and twitching.

At 3, I turned on my light
fumbling for my notepad and favourite pen.

Despite my wife's love
she asked me kindly
to move to the couch
so she could sleep in peace
and where I could write this poem.

Pillow Talk

I had a tussle with my pillow
while making the bed this morning.

As a husband in training,
I attempted to get it into
a flat rectangular pillowcase
packing and pushing
an amorphous lumpy shape
you know, corners into the corners,
like manoeuvring
a fat uncooperative drunk
into a taxicab door.

"Oh, come on,
Can't you fit in, please?"

My grandma always said,
"After rising, you should always make your bed,
it's training for life."
Even research papers have been published
by academics on this subject.

So at the end of your day,
your perfect bed is waiting to greet you
with intoxicating pillow talk,
promising enveloping butterfly kisses
and caressing dreams.

Rock Concert

I left the drapes
and window open
to feel the night air waft in
as you went off
with your girlfriends
to the rock concert.

There was no moon
and I felt you flying back
through the window
with the music,
like Chagall might have painted.
You, floating over soft lapping waves,
and a summer shower tapping lightly
on the big maple leaves.

I didn't know you returned
not even in my sea of dreams.
You came home so late
with a kiss.

In the morning
I saw the text you'd sent
of Florence, singing in the spotlight
running bare foot through the crowd
and everyone screaming.

Sleep Thief

I must have left the kitchen door unlocked
where the sleep thief entered
tip toeing through, ensconcing himself
at the end of my bed.

Damn, him again
that shot of Jameson hadn't worked.

He started unpacking
a hockey bag full of my thoughts
mumbling about my uncertainties and anxieties.

An hour later, he was still there
going on about how much it was raining.

I got impatient, hoping he'd leave soon,
kicking him in the butt hadn't worked.
I tried reading some incomprehensible poetry
and reciting Spanish irregular verbs.

Then I listened to my breathing,
When my girlfriend Dawn arrived
draped in a pink mist
I saw he'd vanished.

It's a Dog's World

Pup Culture

Dog owners are a funny breed
with degrees in pup culture
proud owners of pure breeds, Heinz 57s, rescues
living domesticated in human dog houses.

Rambunctious cuddly puppies
squirming into best friendships,
devoted companions speaking in canine linguistics
a tangible connection to the animal world experts
in the here and now
sniffing out their world.
Are they replacements for children?
Master and student with interchangeable roles.

Walk, walk, who wants to go for a walk?
Where's your leash?
No barking, sit, sit, heel, heel look at me
atta boy, good dog, stay, stay, stay,
fetch, bring the ball, drop, droooop it
roll over, roll over, coobie oobie oobie
atta boy, good Mudgie
look, there goes Brutus and Domino.
Rex, stop sniffing that lady's
leave her alone, come here
Desmond, down boy, down, leave that man's leg alone.

Do they get a sore throat from barking all day?
Oh, Oscar's so smart look at 'em wag his tail
Shake, shake, shake that thing
Winston, don't eat that poo
here's your dinner yum yum
same kibble for the past 12 years,
It's not the dog-eat-dog world here,
with that unique wet fur smell
now you are doing your business,
plastic bag transforms into a cold day hand warmer.

Oh, look at Poopsie she's such a cutie, good dog yes you are
come to Dad atta boy, good dog.
Spot, stop licking that dog's...
come here sit shake a paw
give me a kiss, atta girl
yes, I love you too.

Rover

His fuzzy head hangs out,
paws curled over a red Subaru's back seat window,
stuck in a traffic snarl
looking for dogs in other cars,
curious if any have learned to drive,
ever hopeful for some speed
to flap his ears crazily about.

For now, he's satisfied
his tongue salivating
with the wafting fragrance
from Olive Oil's pizza shop.

In the past he'd thought of running away
to her fragrant palace
but after a serious talk with himself
he will be content at home
lounging on his soft blanket
by the warm stove
unabashedly dangling his legs in mid air
dreaming of catching frisbees.

Morning News

A curly seemingly complacent dog
obediently leashed outside
to a metal chair leg
at her master's favourite coffee shop,
sniffs each patron
watching everything
ever hopeful for a buttery pastry handout
or a friendly ear rub.

At the corner's lamp pole
the bitch has already sniffed this morning's
latest neighbourhood gossip.

In The Dog House

The streetlights are losing to the darkness,
the icy wind chases leaves and tree shadows
as passing ghosts swish over glimmering sidewalks.

There is a distant siren,
a falling tree branch wakes the dog
who starts barking behind a door, alone, afraid, nervous.

He smells the next-door calico going out mousing,
woof, woof, woof;
wait a minute,
there's that cute Dachshund he has a thing for
with her sweet-smelling ass,
out walking with her insomniac owner
who gives a great ear rub
smelling of Jean Paul Gautier.

Being the pick of the litter
and with his owner's patience
he's learned his own name and has translated into his language,
the Concise English Dictionary of Dog Commands;
come, down, heel, sit, stay, roll over, fetch, drop it, good boy.

However, without opposable paws, dang it all,
there's no opening a door handle.

Whimsey

Cracked

Cracked wheat toast
Cracked eggs create a tasty omelette
Cracked pepper spiced it up
Cracked crackers with cheese and dip
Cracks in my face weren't there before
Cracked wine glass threw it out
Cracked child's arm put in a cast
Cracked cell screen, phone didn't die
Cracks in the chassis, dad's car fell apart
Cracked ice on the pond, no more skating
Cracks in the tree trunk, split it apart
Cracks of lightning, starts a forest fire
Cracked plates in the earth's crust, lava erupting
Cracks in the granite mountain, never will heal
Cracks in the clouds, rain comes down
Cracks in the roof, water dripping in
Cracks in the ceiling, drawn like a river
Cracked foundation, grows mould in the home
Cracks in the sidewalk, don't break your mother's back
Cracked plates in the road, Greek New Year's Eve
Cracks in the road, creates an abstract drawing
Crack addict, shoots without hope
Cracked relationship, needs mediation
Crack pot governments, squandering our money
Cracks in my teacup, still makes me happy
Cracks in my heart, my love flows in and out
Cracks all over our world
Cracking me up.

Church Sign

The glassed in sign by the church
cradles the Lord's welcoming message all in capitals,
hopefully applying to you.
"JESUS IS WITH YOU"

The pastor had had an inspiring glass of red,
paging through his Good Book
searching for a biblical insight
of the inextinguishable love of a Mother to her Son.
or a quote from his two beloved pals, Peter and Paul.

Choosing letters from his special box,
he changed it to one of his congregations' favourites.
Standing back, checking his spelling,
CAN'T SLEEP? COUNTING SHEEP? TALK TO THE
GOOD SHEPHERD.

It stares at you on your daily commute,
at the intersection where the light is always red.

Last week the message was
HE WILL SHOW YOU THE WAY
The car radio reported a three car crash on the bridge ahead
Google Maps suggested an alternate route.

This might have been your sign to go to church
not just for family weddings or funerals,
but to find some inner peace,
talk of sins, requests or gratitudes
to the pastor, the Big Guy or His Son.

Then the light turns green and you race off.

Gaggling Seagulls

Relaxing in the bay
on a log salvager's mossy boom,
they sun themselves
confident, romancing the watery magic,
not missing the rain a bit,
bobbing calmly in a haphazard lineup
like a large Italian family
moms, dads, brothers, sisters, uncles, aunts and cousins.

Watching their kids paddle about
squawking to one another
discussing their low tide seafood smorgasbord
wind conditions, whale sightings
sharing tales of gales survived
and overheard seaman jokes.

Like the one about the American seaman
at the urinals noticing that an Irish seaman
had a DY tattooed on his penis
bragging that when it's hard it spells out
his girlfriend's name, Daisy.

It's one of their favourites
the punch line being changed many times
and always gets them chuckling.

Magazine Aisle

At our drug store
while my wife shopped
for beauty perpetuating cosmetics,
I visited the magazine aisle
with it's multifarious characters
displayed on the covers.

Glossy rows stretching into a distant perspective
of archetypal colourful faces
beckoning readers with bold catchy banners,
salacious gossip, the come-hither beauties,
diets, travel, cooking, muscle toning, brain tuning,
parenting, science, sports.
Monthly mental packaged prescriptions for
placating or stimulating our imaginations.

After store hours,
while the night crews polish other rows,
these front pagers discuss details
of truths and lies inside their covers,
then catch some beauty sleep
before the morning's shoppers arrive.

Spinal Tattoo

I met a young lady
in the art gallery café
an Ophelia or Amelia
dressed in tight blue jeans
and a backless tank top
with a poem
tattooed
on her spine
in a
vertical
line
like
drops
of
water
touching
her truth

She said
it threaded
around her heart:
singing
hope
weaving around
both lungs:
breath
compassion
descending to a diamond
in her navel:
clarity
vulnerability
delving down through
her moist mystery:
desire
passion
then back up

to a secret
on her tongue:
kindness
truth
spiralling to her
crimson smiling lips:
happiness
confidence
culminating in a fire inside
her sparkling dark eyes:
growth
trust.
All the while
savouring her green salad
and black coffee.

Though she couldn't see it
she imagined
her poem
her prayer
her art
her life
her world
floating around
like a spinning compass
revolving dancing
in a sinuous vaporous spiral
rising out of her hard days
and softer nights
melting into a mist
on the back of her neck.

Then my wife found me
and walked me away
into the gallery.

Saturday Night Swing

Dimmed lights, fans at full speed
favourite tunes bounce off walls
disco ball twirling coloured sparkles
hot air flying between warmed bodies
shifting left foot, right foot, talking to each other
a light hand on her shoulder blade
hands softly coupling, loving the movement
smiling eyes talking to hot feet
smooth spinning leather soles
stepping with the beat
back on the left, forward on the right
owning the floor, polishing the parquet
a shared three-minute partner
mobile connected embrace embodying enjoyment.

You can't think of your problems tonight
one hand up, round in circles
a soft lash of long hair across my face
don't touch the do
intoxicating movement without alcohol
clothed erotic closeness.

Creative partners in each other's arms,
some move like a chiffon scarf
a tall drink of water
others are jitterbugs
hearts racing, creative partners in each other's arms

The song ends
on a tight beat or fade away
it's over, thanks, connect with another partner
as the next dance begins.

The Ventriloquist At The Beach
(Inspired by a painting by William Isaacs)

A ventriloquist and his Little Buddy
had a whale of an idea,
to go to the beach on their day off.

Carrying their shoes,
feeling the warm sand between their toes,
setting their red and white canvas beach chairs
close to the water's edge
right where the big waves changed
into a flat wash of bubbles.

They arrived for a peaceful break
prepared for the day, with a cooler
suntan cream and
a bottle of appropriate libations.

Settling in with satisfied smiles,
Little Buddy stretched out his arms
letting the warm salt air
blow through his tiny open fingers.

They watched the seagulls
soar and swoop
in a water-coloured sky
as the sea sounds
drowned out their tired memories
of last night's thundering applause
when they cracked
their favourite crowd-pleasing jokes
and couldn't seem to stop talking
about almost everything.

The Juggler At The Beach

Across the hot sands
at the crowded Sunday beach
a juggler brought his balls
with a promise of a show.
A show-off perhaps,
an exhibitionist definitely.

Despite his concentrated face
contentment emanated
from a steady place in his mind.

Controlled repeating rhythms
single handed
two, two
hand to hand, right to left
rising, falling
clockwise, counterclockwise
three, three, three
love of movement from his blurred arms
four, four, four, four
a rare one dropped
then some brief competition
from a pesky Jack Russell
retrieving it, tossing it back in the mix
four, four, four, four
like earthly planets around the sun
five, five, five, five, five
yellow, white, green, red, blue
a confluence of flying balls and rhythmical waves.

He didn't see me
with the balls I juggle.
My own life being tossed around
two, two
tea and toast
three, three, three
cell phone, car keys, glasses
four, four, four, four
relationship, family, friends, the cat
five, five, five, five, five
groceries, emails, note pad, pen, carpentry
dropping the pen
now the cat's playing with it
retrieving it
tossing it back in the mix
five, five, five, five, five
calendar, errands, moods, cooking, rare moments of silence
yellow, white, green, red and blue.

After a swim, he carried on
as the warm racing waves
repeatedly splashed his legs,
caressing his quiet concentration
on the edge of the broad Pacific,
wafting with children's shouts of joy
in breezes of salt and sunscreen,
orbs revolving in an overhead ballet
of curious interest to the local seagulls
soaring swooping circling
checking him out, but preferring
a dropped french fry.

The Pantomime At The Beach

Last Sunday at the beach
I saw a white faced pantomime
tumble out of the bus
with a large bundle
of imaginary summer accoutrements.

Emphatically, he hopped across the scorching sands
and found the perfect spot.

With his articulate, white-gloved hands
and the help from the warm ocean breeze
he unfolded and spread out his illusory towel.

Next, he set up an invisible umbrella,
fretting and fussing,
where it's shade
would be most suitable.

He then reclined on his side,
like a Buddha in repose
and with a calm sigh
fell asleep.

The Clairvoyant Not At The Beach

The clairvoyant was going to go to the beach
to join her friends the ventriloquist
the pantomime
and the juggler.

However, she saw in her crystal ball
they could all get drenched
in an unusual summer shower

So, she stayed at home.

Two Nuns

On a recess from the Convent
two habited nuns
warm rosaries in hand
morning Hail Marys completed
piously and excitedly wait
in a coffee shop line up
with their to-go mugs
and devout faith.

One double white flat cappuccino
and a small mocha
with heavenly whipped cream please.

Perfetto.

The good Lord
understands Italian
and works in amazing ways.

Acknowledgments

Firstly, I'm grateful to my dear friend, Gerald Formosa, whose inspiration blew from the winds of Malta to awaken in me a love of poetry.

A huge thank you to my lovely wife, Trish, for her unending and stimulating support, even though I sometimes had to tie her down to do the editing and to my stepson, Adrian, for patiently assisting with my computer skills.

I've been blessed with a lottery-win of sisters-in-law: Bernadette, Lulu, Cori and notably Grace and her husband David for sharing his publishing expertise.

Thanks to those at the Callanish support group, for buoying me up through dark times and those who listened to after dinner readings, when wine calmed my timidity.

Stimulating encouragements came from good friends: Diane May, whose wisdom bloomed from a rose; Rick Thaller, for my safety diploma; Anwar Selo, Barbara Wiltshire, Judi Gedye, Marcelle O'Reilly, Les Holst, Maria Skeys, Nik Wylie, Rick Downie, Sandi Dunn, Neil Dawe, Isabel Ruediger, Michael Fahy Hawkins, Tom McDonald, Sarah Carley, Wayne Swingle. And, to all of you who have offered help and encouragement whose names do not appear above... a sincere thank you!

Of course, thanks to Bernie Anderson for his contribution to the cover design and Paul Steeves for polishing up my cover photo.

Yes, that's really me blowing up a birthday balloon.

About the Author

As a young boy, John showed very little artistic promise, yet he inherited a curious creative gene from his mother's side and at the age of 24, in the tropics of southern India, began pen and ink illustrations and acrylic surrealist paintings at an ashram, The World Academy of Wonder.

On his return to Vancouver in 1976, he attended Langara College where he acquired a diploma in Fine Arts. He then moved on to Emily Carr University of Art + Design graduating in 1985 in the fascinating world of ceramics. He was commissioned to create ceramic relief murals of sea life for local and international restaurants, businesses and hotels.

John subsidized his sculpting by refinishing yachts, home restoration and finishing carpentry, while concurrently teaching ceramics for ten years with the Vancouver School Board.

In 1996, he met his wife when commissioned to tailor her kitchen cabinets, hence the first section of this volume are poems for his love. Nowadays, John and Trish divide their time between Vancouver and Bowen Island.

In 2019 John put down his skill saw and retired to his man shed. Walking local beaches, he discovered beauty in random pieces of driftwood and transferred his love of ceramic sculpture into creating whimsical wooden vessels with animated clay characters.

Blowing Up Growing Up is John's first published poetry collection.

Manufactured by Amazon.ca
Bolton, ON

43521313R00095